The Battle of Antietam

A Captivating Guide to an Important Battle of the American Civil War

© Copyright 2020

All Rights Reserved. No part of this book may be reproduced in any form without permission in writing from the author. Reviewers may quote brief passages in reviews.

Disclaimer: No part of this publication may be reproduced or transmitted in any form or by any means, mechanical or electronic, including photocopying or recording, or by any information storage and retrieval system, or transmitted by email without permission in writing from the publisher.

While all attempts have been made to verify the information provided in this publication, neither the author nor the publisher assumes any responsibility for errors, omissions or contrary interpretations of the subject matter herein.

This book is for entertainment purposes only. The views expressed are those of the author alone, and should not be taken as expert instruction or commands. The reader is responsible for his or her own actions.

Adherence to all applicable laws and regulations, including international, federal, state and local laws governing professional licensing, business practices, advertising and all other aspects of doing business in the US, Canada, UK or any other jurisdiction is the sole responsibility of the purchaser or reader.

Neither the author nor the publisher assumes any responsibility or liability whatsoever on the behalf of the purchaser or reader of these materials. Any perceived slight of any individual or organization is purely unintentional.

Free Bonus from Captivating History (Available for a Limited time)

Hi History Lovers!

Now you have a chance to join our exclusive history list so you can get your first history ebook for free as well as discounts and a potential to get more history books for free! Simply visit the link below to join.

Captivatinghistory.com/ebook

Also, make sure to follow us on Facebook, Twitter and Youtube by searching for Captivating History.

Contents

FREE BONUS FROM CAPTIVATING HISTORY (AVAILABLE FOR A LIMITED TIME)..5
INTRODUCTION..1
CHAPTER 1 – "YOUNG NAPOLEON"..................................4
CHAPTER 2 – SOUTHERN GENTLEMEN............................13
CHAPTER 3 – THE MEN WHO FOUGHT, THEIR EQUIPMENT AND UNIFORMS..18
CHAPTER 4 – BATTLE OF SOUTH MOUNTAIN AND HARPER'S FERRY..31
CHAPTER 5 – ANTIETAM..41
CHAPTER 6 – DUNKER CHURCH......................................46
CHAPTER 7: "BLOODY LANE"..55
CHAPTER 8: BURNSIDE'S BRIDGE....................................59
CONCLUSION..69
CHECK ANOTHER BOOK BY CAPTIVATING HISTORY ERROR! BOOKMARK NOT DEFINED.
FREE BONUS FROM CAPTIVATING HISTORY (AVAILABLE FOR A LIMITED TIME)..72

Introduction

On September 17th, 1862, US President Abraham Lincoln got the great victory he had desired ever since the outbreak of the American Civil War over a year before. Declaring victory would give him the political breathing space he needed to do something that he had been pondering for some time—freeing the slaves.

The great victory Lincoln wanted took place near Antietam Creek in Maryland, near the town of Sharpsburg. The Union called it "The Battle of Antietam," and the Confederacy referred to it as "The Battle of Sharpsburg." It is known by both today, but "Antietam" is the more common usage.

The thing about the Battle of Antietam was that it wasn't really a victory for either side. It was more like a bloody stalemate, except for the fact that the troops of the North remained near the battlefield while the rebels moved to a position that was more suited for defense.

While the battle certainly was not the resounding victory Lincoln had hoped for, he was a very astute politician. If his troops were still on the field and the enemy was not, he won. Privately, though, Lincoln was both angered and horrified by the results of the battle, or rather the lack of them.

Though there were four battles to come (Gettysburg, Spotsylvania, Chickamauga, and the Wilderness) that were to be more costly in terms of men killed, Antietam, unlike the battles listed above, was fought during the course of one day and was, therefore, the single bloodiest day of the Civil War. And the losses were high—2,100 Union and 1,550 Confederate troops died that day.

Think of this: since 2001, approximately 2,440 American servicemen and women have been killed in the war in Afghanistan. On one single day in 1862, around 158 years ago, that number was exceeded by over one thousand soldiers. That does not take away any of the bravery of the soldiers fighting today; rather, it is simply meant to illustrate the intensity and costliness of the Battle of Antietam.

The Battle of Antietam is remembered today as being the bloodiest day in the Civil War, and as being the "victory" that Lincoln needed to issue the Emancipation Proclamation, but at the time, the reaction to the battle was far from unanimous. Lincoln, members of his Cabinet, Congress, the press, and the public hoped that General George McClellan would take advantage of the situation and pursue the retreating rebels back into Virginia and to their capital, Richmond. But as he had done so many times before, McClellan hesitated, coming up with reason after reason about why he could not chase the rebels down.

So, a short biography of George McClellan is a good place to begin this history of the Battle of Antietam.

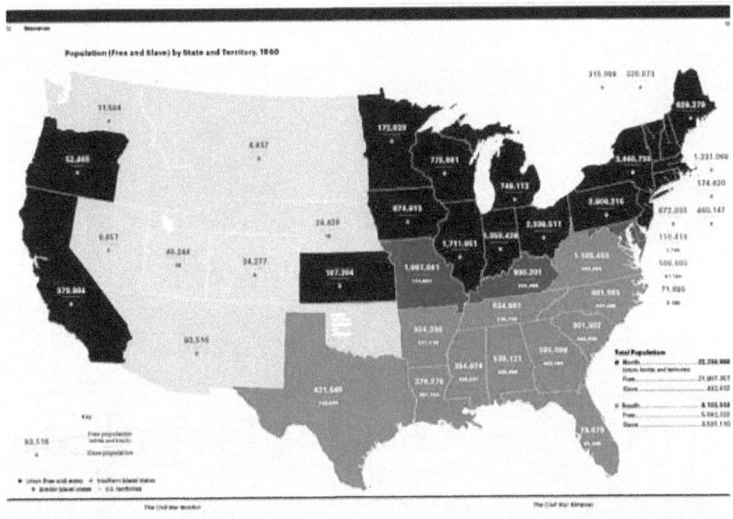

Illustration 1: Free and Slave States and their populations in 1861

Chapter 1 – "Young Napoleon"

In the mid-19th century, the idol of military men throughout the Western world was Napoleon Bonaparte. Even though he was ultimately defeated, he had taken on the world, almost won, and had done it in a way that hadn't been seen on the battlefield before. Audacity, speed, and surprise were the hallmarks of Napoleon's military career.

In the United States, which hadn't felt the brunt of Napoleon's invading armies, Napoleon was revered. Look at the pictures of the officers (and some of the enlisted men) of the Civil War—they pose like Bonaparte, with one hand tucked into his jacket, like the picture of Union General George McClellan below.

The nickname "Young Napoleon" was given to him as he rose to take command of the Army of the Potomac, the main Union Army in the eastern theater of the Civil War, after a couple of small victories in western Virginia (in today's West Virginia, which was separated from Virginia in 1863).

At the time, the nickname, while bold, made more sense than it would later in the war. McClellan, who was born in Philadelphia in December 1826, had a stellar career before gaining control of the Army of the Potomac: he was second in the 1846 West Point class (which included future Confederate generals Stonewall Jackson, George Pickett, and A.P. Hill), distinguished himself in the Mexican-American War, returned to teach at West Point, led mapping expeditions on the frontier and explored routes for the transcontinental railroad, and went overseas as a military observer in the Crimean War.

In the years before the Civil War, McClellan had retired to private life and became an executive with the Illinois Central Railroad. There, he made important connections, including with the governor of Ohio, William Dennison Jr., who appointed McClellan as the major general of Ohio volunteers in 1861 shortly after the war began in April 1861. This promotion from private life to one of the highest ranks in the army brought McClellan to the attention of President Lincoln, who also received positive reviews about McClellan from the Ohio governor. Lincoln promoted McClellan to major general, a position that was right below Mexican-American War hero Winfield Scott, on whose staff McClellan had served in that war.

In the first truly planned action of the war (as opposed to incidental skirmishes) at Philippi in western Virginia in June 1861, McClellan's troops were victorious. Though small in scale compared to what was to come, the victory at Philippi (involving some four thousand men on both sides) reinforced the Northern notion that the war would be short. Naturally, the people in the South felt the same way at the beginning of the war.

The Battle of Philippi was also the first indicator to President Lincoln that McClellan was going to be a problem. Though McClellan wasn't announcing anything different than what was standing government policy in 1861, in western Virginia, he announced to the populace that his army would not interfere with slavery in the area. Answering rumors that the Union troops would encourage slave revolt, McClellan announced, "not only will we abstain from all such interference but we will, on the contrary with an iron hand, crush any attempted insurrection on their part." This was not within McClellan's authority to announce or enforce without orders, as those orders were supposed to come from the civilian authority—meaning Lincoln. McClellan quickly apologized to the president, but it was the first of many, and other apologies would come much slower with time, if at all.

Over a month after McClellan's fight in western Virginia, the Union lost the First Battle of Bull Run under General Irvin McDowell. With that shocking defeat, Lincoln began searching for a new commander of the Union armies in Virginia. Not only was McClellan appointed to head the Army of the Potomac, but he was also made the commander of all Union forces.

It became clear almost immediately that McClellan had a gift for organization, discipline, and instilling pride in his troops, all of which were lacking since the beginning of the war and especially after the First Battle of Bull Run. Though there were still problems in the quartermaster corps (the branch of the service responsible for the requisitioning and distribution of supplies), such as officers selling army goods for their own private gain, making sure their friends in the army got first choice, and bribery, McClellan and his staff went a long way to fixing the worst of the problems.

The general fired inefficient, lazy, and inept officers and had them sent into retirement or assigned to desk jobs or posts far from any action, and he also brought up new officers that were familiar with modern tactics, drills, and organization. McClellan made sure that discipline was enforced, which, deep down, most troops love—no one wants to go to battle with a mob of undisciplined men, especially when facing a skilled enemy. In time, the men loved McClellan, for while it was a fatal flaw in regard to his career, his cautiousness meant, at least to average soldiers, that "Little Mac" would not throw their lives away on a whim and without preparation.

McClellan was no stranger to what we today would call "spin." He courted the leading newspapermen of the day, was the toast of Washington society, and made political connections wherever he could. Soon, the newspapers, his men, and much of the Northern public was calling him the "Young Napoleon." McClellan did nothing to dissuade them.

And that right there was one of McClellan's biggest problems—his massive ego. He feigned modesty when he was called the "Young Napoleon," but deep down, many believe that he enjoyed it immensely and that it went to his head, which was already large from being second in his West Point class (he was bested by one point because of an athletic event) and having won some early, but small, victories in western Virginia.

As the war went on, Lincoln and others began to realize that McClellan was way too cautious for a general in command of a powerful army and perhaps was more concerned with not losing his army or reputation rather than winning victories. McClellan would not take this laying down, though; the general began describing Lincoln and his Cabinet in increasingly disparaging terms. He had to know reports of this would get back to Washington, DC, but he seemingly didn't care or incredibly did not know.

McClellan's first grand idea culminated in the Peninsula Campaign, an amphibious landing on the James Peninsula, which was south of Richmond and behind Confederate positions facing Washington. It was a great idea in many ways. It could possibly surprise the enemy. It also ensured that McClellan's Army of the Potomac, numbering in the neighborhood of 100,000 men during the summer of 1862, would be concentrated in a small area, which would allow them to bear down on the rebels with great force while having, at least for a time, the cover of the US Navy's guns. Conversely, however, the territory would also allow a smaller enemy led by skilled officers to keep the larger enemy bottled up. It all depended on leadership and boldness, the latter trait being something McClellan did not have.

At Yorktown, where the American Revolution ended, McClellan besieged a smaller CSA ("Confederate States of America") army under General John B. Magruder. Instead of maneuvering to defeat him or simply (in the parlance of WWII) "kick ass and bypass," McClellan left the much weaker force behind him to be "cleaned" up by US troops coming up from behind while McClellan pressed on toward Richmond.

Magruder shrewdly maneuvered his troops in sight of the Federal forces (another name used to refer to the Union) so they thought the rebels were much more numerous than they were. He also employed Quaker guns to make the Union general believe he had more artillery than he truly did. The phrase Quaker guns is a play on words, as the religious Quaker sect espouses to this day non-violence. These "guns" were actually logs painted black and leaned against rocks or set up on wheels in plain (but distant) sight of the enemy. Magruder had dozens of these "guns" deployed in the field.

Magruder also had spies and scouts, and the Confederates had double agents within the Federal camps and in Washington, spreading rumors about the immense strength of the Confederate forces. Of course, these were all gross exaggerations, as the Confederate forces in Virginia were outnumbered by the Union Army.

One of the most interesting things (and one of the most tragic in many ways) about the Civil War was that many of the officers knew each other, even if they were on the opposing side. Sometimes they were best friends, as in the case of Confederate General Lewis Armistead and Union General Winfield Scott Hancock. Whether they knew each other as friends, acquaintances, family, or just by reputation, many of the men who fought in the Civil War had served in the US Army before. That gave them a lot of insight into the tactical and strategic thinking of their enemy.

As mentioned above, McClellan had gone to West Point with some of the South's leading generals. He had also served in Mexico and was known to others, including Robert E. Lee. Most of them knew of McClellan's cautious nature before the war, and they played off of it during the conflict.

Urged to move by Lincoln during the Peninsula Campaign, McClellan began what was to become his ignominious trademark—asking for more troops. He had been supplied with the largest standing army in the history of the North American continent, and he still asked for more men, men that didn't exist. The draft wasn't instituted until 1863, and until that time, Washington was dependent on volunteers, and these men took time to train and outfit.

Lincoln complained about McClellan's lack of movement, which was made worse not only by the claims of Southern strength (which Lincoln, from his intelligence sources, likely knew to be an exaggeration) but also by McClellan's assurances that when he was ready, he would move with great speed. President Lincoln famously said, "If General McClellan is not using the army, perhaps he might let me borrow it." Just before the Peninsula Campaign, Lincoln removed McClellan from overall command of the Union armies, hoping that the general might be able to focus on the upcoming campaign near Richmond better. While McClellan seems to have known that he was out of his depth as the commander of all the Union forces, he still harbored resentment against someone who he believed knew nothing of military planning.

McClellan had written to his wife that he viewed Lincoln as "a well-meaning baboon." To McClellan, Secretary of State William Seward, who was 25 years older than the general, was an "incompetent little puppy."

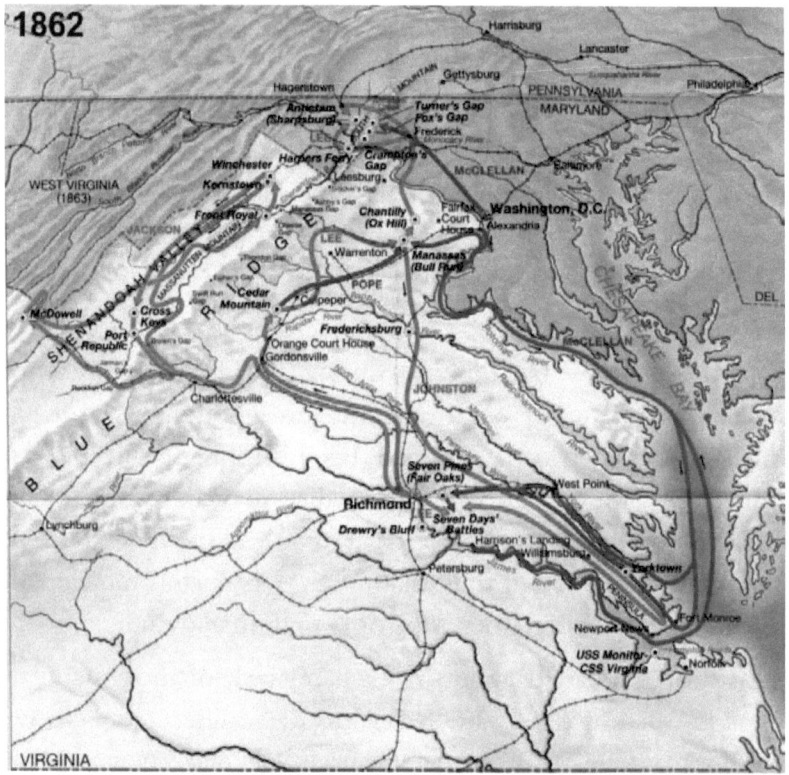

Illustration 1: The Campaigns in the East through fall 1862

Before the Peninsula Campaign began, Lincoln, Seward, and Lincoln's private secretary John Hay paid a late-night visit to the McClellan residence to discuss the general's plans for the upcoming campaign. Informed that the general was out, Lincoln and his party decided to wait. A bit later, McClellan came in by another door and went upstairs to bed, despite being informed that the president of the United States and the secretary of state were waiting in his parlor. A half-hour went by before a servant came down and explained to the president that the general had "gone to bed." John Hay felt that the president should be incensed, but Lincoln only replied that is was "better at this time not to be making points of etiquette and personal dignity." He never visited McClellan's home again, though.

During the Seven Days' Battles at the end of the Peninsula Campaign, McClellan's armies, when they were engaged, fought well. Actually, they won more battles than they lost. However, they were outmaneuvered and fooled throughout the campaign into thinking the Confederate Army was much bigger than their own. By the end of the three-month campaign, which lasted from March to July 1862, the Union troops were dejected, and they were loaded on boats and sent home to Washington.

McClellan had been outmaneuvered and fooled by a new Confederate commander, as the old one, Joseph E. Johnston, had been wounded in the Battle of Seven Pines. The new commander of the Army of Northern Virginia, the main force of the CSA, was Robert E. Lee. At the end of the Peninsula Campaign, Lincoln relieved McClellan of his command, sending him into semi-retirement.

This enforced retirement would not last long, however. At the Second Battle of Bull Run (also known as the Second Battle of Manassas, which is what it was/is more commonly called in the South) in late August, McClellan's replacement, General John Pope, was routed by Robert E. Lee, and the Army of the Potomac was once again sent into disarray, as it had been after the First Battle of Bull Run.

In September, Lincoln reluctantly called McClellan back to duty, appointing him commander of "the fortifications of Washington, and all the troops for the defense of the capital." By this time, McClellan's caution, ego, and caustic pen and tongue had alienated the Cabinet as well, for all of them urged Lincoln not to reappoint "Little Mac." Lincoln admitted that reappointing McClellan was like curing a hangover with "the hair of the dog," but he told his secretary, "We must use what tools we have. There is no man in the Army who can man these fortifications and lick these troops of ours into shape half as well as he. If he can't fight himself, he excels in making others ready to fight."

So it was that George McClellan was in command of the Union armies in Virginia when Robert E. Lee devised his first plan for an incursion into the North to force "the Yankees" into a negotiated peace.

Chapter 2 – Southern Gentlemen

Where McClellan was cautious, Robert E. Lee was bold, as were most of his generals, most notably Thomas J. "Stonewall" Jackson. They were brought up in the Southern military tradition, hearkening back to the Revolutionary War days of Nathanael Greene, the American commander who, though a Northerner, fought a classic campaign against the more numerous British in the South.

Southern officers were also inculcated with the notion of honor and chivalry, and many sons of the Confederacy were brought up on tales of knights charging through enemy lines to save the day. And lastly, just like McClellan and many Northern officers, they idolized the military career of Napoleon Bonaparte and his audacious and revolutionary tactics. Unlike McClellan, though, they put them into action much more often.

Of course, the most famous man in the South was Robert E. Lee. Though he had lost a number of battles to McClellan in the Seven Days' Battles, he was so skillful in maneuvering his troops that he not only caused McClellan to retreat back to Washington, but he also convinced many in the North that his army was nigh to invincible—which, for a short time, it was.

But that reputation was to come after the Seven Days' Battles and after the subject of this book, the Battle of Antietam. Lee was to go on and win decisive victories at Fredericksburg and Chancellorsville in 1863 before moving on to his second incursion in the North at Gettysburg. There, he would sustain the defeat that many consider to be the turning point in the war, but even after that battle, and despite his seeming lack of judgment in ordering Pickett's suicidal charge, Lee caused US General Ulysses S. Grant much frustration in the defensive battles in Virginia until the war's end.

Lee had been offered the command of all Union armies after the Battle of Fort Sumter, the battle that started off the Civil War. He had already distinguished himself at West Point, both as a student and an instructor, in the Mexican-American War, and in the projects he had undertaken in the Corps of Engineers after that conflict. Lee was the man in charge of the Virginia militia that put down John Brown's anti-slavery rebellion at Harper's Ferry and was one of the most well-known and respected men in the US military, as well as the country in general.

But Lee's first loyalty was to the state of Virginia, which he (and many other Virginians) called their "home country." In those days, most people never traveled outside of their county unless they were in the army or navy, and they had very little contact with Washington, DC, or people from outside their state or even immediate area. Railroads were beginning to change that, albeit slowly, and it didn't really impact most of the people in the South, as railroad production there lagged far behind the North (which came to be a big factor in the Civil War), and the price to ride the rails was prohibitive for many. So, Lee, like many other Southerners, counted his loyalty to his state first and the Union second, especially when it came to the government telling them how to live.

Illustration 2: Colorized picture of Lee in his Confederate uniform. Source unknown

Of course, the main issue of the Civil War was slavery, though many at the time said that the issue was states' rights, an opinion that is still held today by some. Lee is hard to pin down on the issue of slavery in some ways. He was a slave owner and is recorded as having administered harsh punishments. He is also recorded to have set slaves free, and like some other leading Southerners, Lee believed that slavery would die a natural death. However, it wasn't up to the men in the North, who had no idea how much slavery was a part of both economic and social life (according to Southern thinking), to tell Southerners what to do with their "property."

Lee turned down Lincoln's offer, crossed the river to Virginia, then went to the Virginia Legislature and accepted their offer to lead the armies of Virginia, which were forming at that moment.

One of those units that were forming was the Virginia Military Institute Corps of Cadets, led by Major Thomas Jackson, soon to be known to all as "Stonewall." Jackson had been at West Point as well, graduating in 1846 with George McClellan, among others who would fight alongside and against him in the Civil War.

Many people familiar with the Civil War know that Jackson was what some might call an "odd duck." He burned with Christian religious fervor, yet when faced with the aftermath of the looting in Fredericksburg, Virginia, by Union forces, he wanted to "kill 'em all." Jackson often rode his horse or walked about with one hand in the air so as to "keep himself in balance." He sometimes would hold his leg out of the stirrup for the same reason. Most famously, he often sucked on lemons, which is a good idea when scurvy was a real danger, but he was often seen with a lemon in his mouth while riding or even during battle. Jackson wouldn't eat pepper because he thought it weakened his left leg, and he wouldn't send letters that would be in transit on the Sabbath but fought many of his greatest battles on Sunday. In his teaching tenure, he brooked no talking in class. One of his students, James Walker, who ironically would become a brigadier general under Jackson at Antietam, challenged Stonewall to a duel because Jackson singled him out for talking in class, an accusation that Walker believed to be false.

All was forgiven by the time of the Civil War, as Walker's testimony in Jackson's disciplinary hearing illustrates the view of most of the cadets that Jackson taught: "Major Jackson is a stranger [author's note: meaning "strange"] amongst us and brings from the field of his late brilliant achievements many singular and eccentric notions."

By the time of the Battle of Antietam, Jackson's eccentricities had partially endeared him to his men, and his victories, which included the First Battle of Bull Run, the Shenandoah

Illustration 3: Jackson at VMI 1857 (Courtesy VMI Museum)

Campaign, and the Second Battle of Bull Run, had made him famous throughout the South.

As we discuss the Battle of Antietam and the events leading up to it, we will introduce you to other leading figures, both from the South and the North.

Chapter 3 – The Men Who Fought, Their Equipment and Uniforms

Most of the time when we read of the Civil War, we read about the men we've mentioned above or other leaders, like Ulysses S. Grant or William Tecumseh Sherman. Though there are books and movies that do talk about the lives of the average soldier, they seem to be few and far between. So, let's take a little time to talk about the men who did the bulk of the fighting and most of the dying in the American Civil War.

If you look at the old hurried films of the beginning of World War I in nations throughout Europe, crowds seem to be going crazy at the prospect of war. Today, when a nation is attacked, as in the case of 9/11, a grim determination sets in, and perhaps there is talk about how quickly the enemy will be beaten, but there is seldom joy. At the start of WWI, as you can see in those films, the people in the crowds when war was announced or when the soldiers began to march off actually seemed happy. Of course, we know that they learned very quickly that WWI was going to be very different than anything anyone had experienced in history before, and that joy turned into grief and anger very quickly.

The Civil War was the same way. There are famous tales of crowds riding out to Manassas Junction, Virginia, from Washington, DC, to see what they expected to be a "grand sight," to use the parlance of the time. Many believed the Federal Army would rout the Southerners in one quick go. As the men in (mostly) blue came running back from the front lines, some of them with arms, hands, and eyes hanging off, those same crowds panicked, and at least some of them began to realize their ideas about a glorious war might be incorrect.

The men who initially fought felt the same way, at least those who had not done any fighting, which was most of them. Most of the men in the army who had fought in the Mexican-American War were either officers or retired, and there was a limited number of non-commissioned officers who had done some fighting on the frontier. However, most of the men who filled the ranks of the "Blue and the Gray" had no idea what they were getting into.

By the time the war began in 1861, people on both sides had known it was coming for some time. A civil war had almost happened during the "nullification crisis" of 1832-33, and tensions flared up again during the years before the war in a low-level guerrilla war in Kansas over the spread of slavery. The "nullification crisis" involved radicals from the South, who were led by Southern firebrand John C. Calhoun. Calhoun and others believed that President Andrew Jackson and the federal government were taking too much power for themselves, and they asserted that states had the right to "nullify" any federal law they found ran contrary to the laws of their states or wishes of their legislature. Jackson threatened an invasion of Calhoun's home state of South Carolina, and so, the "nullifiers" backed down, but the tensions between the Southern states and the federal government would remain.

One of the many sad things about the Southern cause was that many of the men in the rank and file had more in common with their Northern brethren working in factories and, to an extent, slaves than they did to their officers. The poor whites of the South were largely illiterate and barely educated. They fell to sickness with great regularity, considering the climate and the state of hygiene and health in the 19th century. The upper classes in the South held most of the power, and a relatively small number of families in each state or county held most of that power.

Though there was some upward social mobility in the South, the agricultural nature of the Southern economy did not allow the same social climbing that happened in the North. There were, of course, exceptions, such as in the case of Nathan Bedford Forrest, who built a fortune trading slaves.

Still, the men of the South who filled the ranks of the Confederate armies could hold themselves above somebody—the slaves. And the Southerners were full of resentment toward the Northerners, who believed they could tell Southerners how to run their lives.

For the men of the North, the issue was unity. A sizable minority did care about the slavery issue, and more began to care as they moved into the South and saw the conditions that the vast majority of slaves lived in, but maintaining the unity of the fairly new nation, which wasn't even one hundred years old yet, was their main cause. To them, the Southerners were betraying what the American Revolution had been fought for, what many of their forefathers had died for. Additionally, many Northern officers, after having been stationed in the South, realized the very class-conscious and increasingly outdated Southern society, seeing in it shades of the very aristocracy the men of the Revolution had fought against.

Of course, there were men on both sides who simply fought because that's what their countrymen were doing; they didn't want to be accused of cowardice or of not being a patriot. Some joined for the adventure. Many new immigrants in both parts of the country joined to prove themselves Americans. And some simply joined for a paycheck.

Weapons and Equipment

What did the men of North and South go to war with? As opposed to today's American soldier, who many times goes into the field with eighty or more pounds, carrying everything from ammunition to basic medical equipment, technology, and MREs, the Civil War soldier, for the most part, carried the bare minimum into battle. As a rule, the soldiers were never far from their supply trains, and if they were, they were notorious scroungers—especially the Northern soldiers in the final campaigns of the war.

Generally speaking, the Union soldier was better outfitted than his Southern cousin. As you can see in the following picture, the Northern foot soldier went into battle or on the march carrying a wool blanket atop his knapsack. In that knapsack was his half of a two-man tent, a groundsheet, an overcoat, and personal effects, such as a Bible, razor, sewing kit, etc. He carried his rifle, a forty round cartridge box, a sheathed bayonet, a box for the caps used for firing his weapon (in the early stages of the war), a leather haversack, a cloth-covered canteen, and a tin cup. Of course, this was the average load for the Union soldier—each man made it his own according to his preference and the forbearance of his officers.

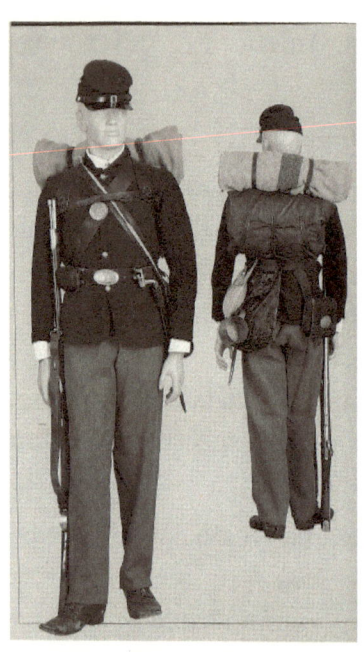

Illustration 4: Standard Union uniform and equipment, later war

Unfortunately for the men of both sides, their uniforms were made of wool. Not only was this hot in the summer, but it was also itchy. Linen blouses helped somewhat. The Union soldier wore boots or shoes with a square toe, sometimes referred to as "gunboats." The standard issue by the end of the war was a blue uniform, though throughout the war and especially at the beginning, many units (coming as they did from state militias of different traditions and histories) wore various different uniforms, and the colors, hats, and pants varied greatly, as you can see below.

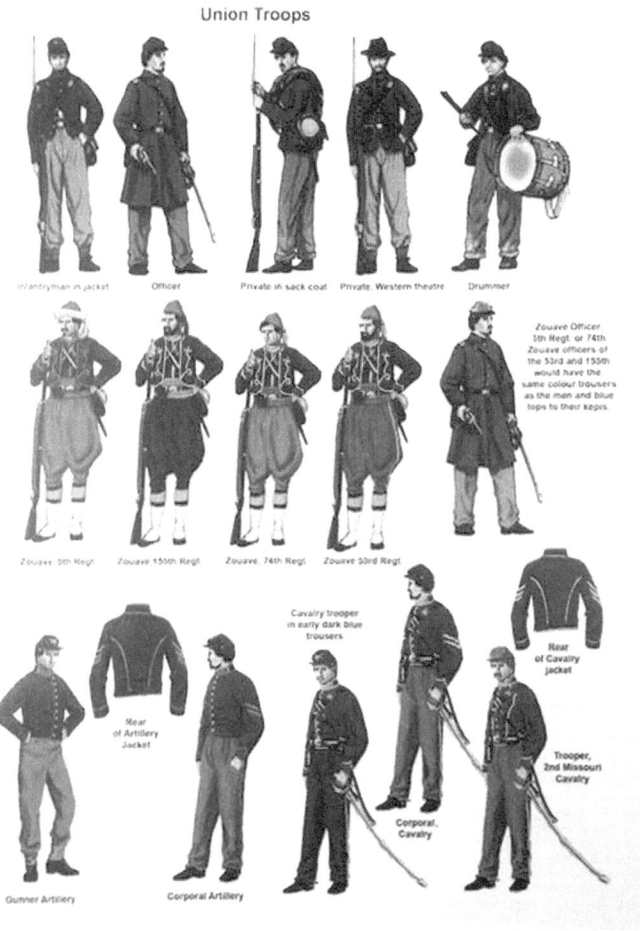

Illustration 5: Various Union regimental, officers', and other uniforms

Though the Confederates had a great deal of variety in their uniforms to start the war, much as the Union men did, by the end of the war, the standard Confederate uniform was either grayish or butternut. In the 1930s, President Franklin Delano Roosevelt honored the survivors of the Civil War by beginning his speech, "Veterans of the Blue and the Gray," but it's more likely that most men in the Confederate armies wore butternut or a mix of both.

Illustration 6: Typical Southern soldier

As you can see from the following picture, the Confederate soldier was generally not as well equipped as his Northern counterpart. This only got worse as the war went on, as the Union would blockade the main Southern ports and take more Southern territory.

Though many Southern soldiers wore the same style of forage hat, or "kepi" as the Northerners, it was gray. Many rebel soldiers wore variations of the slouch hat you see above. Like the Yankees, the rebels wore a jacket covering a linen shirt and occasionally an overcoat. In the winter campaign of 1862, which culminated in the bloody Union defeat at Fredericksburg, many of the Southern soldiers did not even have shoes, let alone overcoats. Southern soldiers often took better clothing off dead Union soldiers or prisoners of war.

"Johnny Reb," as the common Southern soldier was referred to in both the North and the South, carried a blanket slung over his shoulder and maybe a groundsheet or shelter-half, a partial tent, if he was lucky. Oftentimes these were wrapped around extra articles of clothing, such as socks or gloves. Naturally, he carried his weapon, cartridges, cap box, and usually a wooden canteen. Additionally, the Southern soldier often carried a knife in addition to his bayonet.

When the war began, both sides were armed with virtually the same weapons, which meant that capturing the enemy's stores was exceedingly important, especially for the rebels, as most of the weapons production was in the Northern states. As the war went on, blockading the Southern coastline and cutting their supply lines was important to the North in order to prevent what weapons the South could buy overseas or make themselves from getting to their men on the front.

In a book of this length, we are limited to talking about the basics and what most men were equipped with. Let's start with the most common infantry weapon of the war, the Springfield Model 1861. The first long gun to equip iron sights as a standard feature, the Model 1861 was a .58 caliber gun firing a Minié Ball— think about that for a moment. The American heavy machine gun of World War II and today is the Browning .50 caliber. It will tear or blow a man apart. Anti-aircraft carriers of WWII mounted four of these guns on a single mount, and though it was technically "illegal" to use against men, it was done all the time. Its nickname was the "Meatgrinder." Now, think of hundreds of .58 caliber guns all aiming at much the same point, which is what happened during the Civil War. It is no wonder that Antietam remains one of the bloodiest days in US history.

Illustration 7: The conical bullets are Minié balls, the other musket balls. These were found recently on a Civil War battlefield. Notice the aerodynamic shape of the Minié compared to the musket ball.

The ammunition of the Springfield 1861 was the Minié ball, pictured above. As you can see from the spelling, the name has nothing to do with the size of the projectile (and it's clearly not a ball). It was named after its inventor, Claude-Étienne Minié, who designed the French Minié rifle used in the Crimean War.

To fire the 1861 Springfield, as well as other muzzle loading weapons, with the Minié ball, the soldier poured gunpowder down the barrel of the gun (this was a proscribed amount, though more or less could be added for range), then sent the ball down the barrel until it rested on the gunpowder at the bottom. In the case of the Minié ball, the hollowed end allowed the powder to be packed into the bullet rather than around it, as with a musket ball. This also meant that the bottom of the ball flared out and lodged itself in the rifled grooves of the barrel, which, when fired, would send the projectile spinning.

For those of you unfamiliar with firearms, "rifling" means that the inside of the barrel was etched with spiral grooves. In the case of the Minié ball, when the thinner bottom of the cartridge flared out, it provided a block of the gases that propelled the ball. This was different than the older musket ball, which lost power with gases escaping around the sides of the ball as it traveled down the barrel. The rifling of the barrel and the spin put on the projectile meant that rifles (as opposed to the smoothbore musket used previously) had greater range and were much more accurate.

This is one reason why the formation fighting that took place during the Civil War was so deadly. Previously, men grouped together because smoothbore muskets were notoriously inaccurate. Grouping together allowed them to multiply the effect of their weapons and perhaps hit *something*. What the men of the Civil War (especially the officers) did not realize was that with rifling, those formations were essentially a slow-moving target that could hardly be missed. Add the Minié ball and the size of the caliber, and the battlefields of the Civil War were butcher's yards.

A well-trained soldier could fire the Springfield three times a minute. Its effective range was just under three hundred yards, give or take. The rifle was just under 56 inches long and weighed a bit over 9.5 pounds.

Before the mass production of the Springfield, both sides of the war used the British-made Enfield 1853, which was, in most respects, just like the Springfield, except it was manufactured overseas. This would become problematic during the war, especially for the South, not to mention they were fairly expensive.

In the war's last year, breech-loading rifles, carbines (shorter-barreled and lighter rifles, mostly for cavalry use), and repeating rifles were used by some units of the Union Army. Breech-loading meant the projectile, now with powder contained in the cartridge, was inserted at the base of the barrel, meaning no powder pouring or ramming was needed. The advent of the repeating rifle meant that multiple cartridges could be loaded into the weapon and fired one after the other, only stopping to reload a clip of bullets. Obviously, this gave the Union Army a great advantage over the Confederate soldiers, whose own experiments with breech-loading rifles were abortive.

As was mentioned, the men carried a variety of arms, especially at the beginning of the war. This held true for officers and their sidearms as well. Most officers, at least for dress or formal situations, still wore a sword, and some (especially in the cavalry) wore it in battle.

Most Union officers (and some Confederates) carried the Colt M1861 Navy .36 caliber six-shot pistol. The effective range of this gun was between 75 to 100 yards, though most times when the pistol was employed, action was at much closer range. About 40,000 Model 1861s were produced during the war. Many Confederate officers carried a similar weapon, the Colt Model 1860, which was larger in caliber—.44, just like the character Dirty Harry in the movie *Magnum Force* (1973).

The large caliber and relatively slow velocity of Civil War firearms combined with the use of the Minié ball meant that a great deal of damage was done when a soldier was hit. Usually, the ball flattened out when entering the body, and if it didn't hit bone, it continued its way out, usually creating a large exit wound.

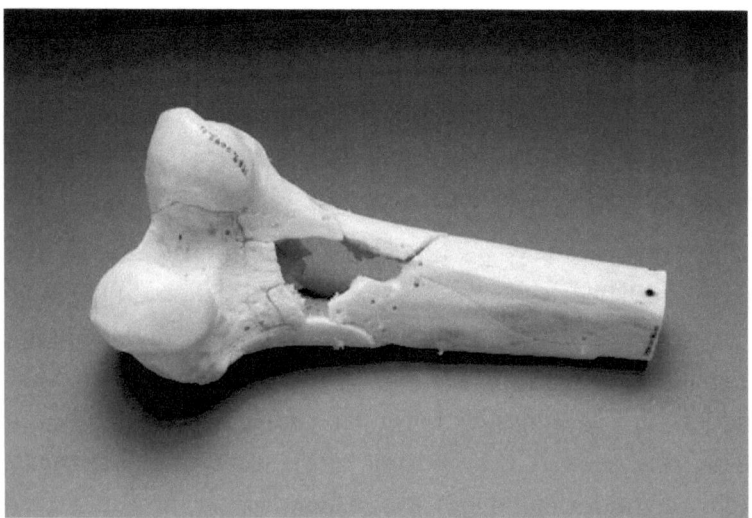

Illustration 9: Upper thigh (femur) hit by Minié ball

Obviously, there were a great many ways to die on the Civil War battlefields. Aside from the weapons described above, artillery in its various forms caused many deaths. However, most of the deaths of the Civil War came not from battlefield injuries but from diseases and post-operative infections.

One of the most famous images of the Civil War is that of the battlefield hospital and the amazing number of amputations done there. Personal accounts of the war and some extant photographs describe and show mountains of arms, legs, hands, and feet cut off in order to save a life. Unfortunately, through most of the war, cleanliness wasn't only next to impossible; its importance wasn't yet realized.

Dirty instruments, hands, bandages, floors, and bedding all meant that many of the men who had survived the battlefield, even with relatively minor wounds, were all in danger of dying from infection. It was not until the US Sanitary Commission, which was formed in 1861 and included many influential and powerful women, lobbied Congress and the military that conditions in the battlefield hospitals began to change, leading to a drop in infection rates, at least in the North. This was also at a time when the idea of germs was just taking hold, and only those at the cutting edge of medical knowledge began to accept the idea.

Those were some of the ways a man could die during the war. But what kept him alive? Well, their field rations—those carried by the men or by units nearby on the march—were hardtack and salt pork. Hardtack is essentially a biscuit or a cracker made from water and flour. Sometimes salt is added. The resultant "hard" cracker has an exceedingly long shelf life, but it is relatively flavorless and could almost break teeth unless softened with more water.

Salt pork is just that—pork salted to preserve it for long periods of time to prevent spoilage. Both of these items increased thirst, which was never a good thing in a situation where water was limited, the weather sometimes hot, and the uniforms made of wool. In camp, the menu varied, but bacon was a staple and a favorite. This was not the healthiest diet, but it wasn't all that different from what they ate at home. Salt and sugar were the prime ways people added flavor and preserved food back then.

Of course, as there have been in all armies throughout history and the world, there were the men skilled at "scrounging"—finding things to add to meals, whether this was done by hunting, wheeling and dealing, or stealing. A good scrounger helped keep men's spirits up, and many Civil War era diaries are filled with tales of men getting their fill of chicken, turkey, deer, and, of course, some kind of alcohol while sitting by the campfire, playing cards, and singing songs.

Toward the end of the war, with much of the South's agricultural land taken over, its ports blockaded, and its railways cut or occupied, starvation set in for both the armies of the Confederate and civilians. Though many Southern armies had a good reputation for not "foraging" (a polite word for "stealing"), whether in its campaigns in the North or at home, in the last year of the war, desperate times called for desperate measures. Many Southern civilians also began to hide what little they had from their own armies.

Obviously, as we know from the tales of "Sherman's March to the Sea" and other episodes, Union troops in the South were notorious for pillaging and raiding Southern farms and homes, especially if they were plantations, as they were the very symbol of the Southern aristocracy.

Chapter 4 – Battle of South Mountain and Harper's Ferry

Throughout the Civil War, General McClellan's reputation went from bad to worse. Much of this had to do with his caution, which may have cost the country tens of thousands of more lives. At times, McClellan had the means and opportunity to win the war, but his fear of losing rather than risking everything to win prolonged the conflict by years.

Adding to McClellan's bad reputation was the discovery of his private letters and writings, as well as contemporary accounts of his comments on Lincoln, the Cabinet, the conduct of the war, and his boasting about his military acumen. Adding to that was his running for president in 1864 on the Democratic ticket and calling for a negotiated peace with the South.

However, as was stated, McClellan may have been a braggart and overly cautious, but he did know something about battles. He did win, though he could have won bigger, and he did rebuild the army twice. Historians have stated that the best use of McClellan's talents would have been as a staff officer or at the head of the Quartermaster Corps, where he likely would have excelled.

Still, in the prelude to the Battle of Antietam, McClellan won a battle that is much overlooked by history—the Battle of South Mountain. But the Union also lost an important battle in the time just before Antietam at Harper's Ferry.

The Battle of South Mountain took place in the hills of western Maryland, near the area where Camp David lies today. In early September 1862, Robert E. Lee, fresh off the Confederate victories at the Second Battle of Bull Run and Jackson's Shenandoah Campaign, launched an invasion of Maryland with the ultimate goals of taking pressure off Richmond, cutting Union supply lines to Washington from the "breadbasket" of Pennsylvania, and perhaps forcing Lincoln to a negotiated peace. Lee's broader goal was the seizure of the capital of Pennsylvania at Harrisburg, an important river port at the time, but to do that, he would have to make his way through Maryland first and reduce the Federal garrison at Harper's Ferry, located in western Virginia.

The Union garrison at Harper's Ferry contained some 14,000 men and significant amounts of artillery. It was meant to be a check on any rebel moves northward and to keep the confluence of the Shenandoah and Potomac Rivers clear of rebel interference. It was a very strong force, and in the right hands, it could have stalled or perhaps stopped any Confederate drive north into Pennsylvania.

However, in command of the Harper's Ferry garrison was Colonel Dixon Miles, who, among other things, was likely an alcoholic. He was also eccentric and aging, though the two might not have been mutually exclusive. He had developed the odd habit of wearing two hats at a time—the reason is lost to history, but perhaps he simply didn't remember the first one was there.

Harper's Ferry was familiar to Lee and Jackson. They were both native Virginians, and Jackson had grown up in the western part of the state. He was present when John Brown and his comrades were hanged after Lee put down the rebellion at Harper's Ferry, commanding a contingent of Virginia Military Institute cadets sent there to help keep order.

One good thing about the town of Harper's Ferry itself is that it commands the local river traffic. Unfortunately, it is also surrounded by steep hills and cliffs, giving any commander determined enough to get cannons on them a decided advantage. Miles was determined, but he only placed a few guns and two thousand men on the most tactically important heights, known as Maryland Heights, and left nearby Loudoun Heights undefended. He chose to place most of his men to the west, convinced that the rebels were going to attack across the flat plains to the west of the town.

Lee knew that he would have to eliminate or bottle up the forces at Harper's Ferry if he wanted to advance farther north. What he did was to become his trademark in later battles: he divided his weaker forces to engage the enemy where he was least expected, with both audacity and speed. Lee sent Stonewall Jackson, who commanded about 30,000 men, to take care of Harper's Ferry, while he moved with the rest of his army, about 20,000 men, in the direction of Hagerstown, Maryland.

Over the course of the next three days (September 12th-15th), Jackson moved his artillery and most of his men into the hills surrounding Harper's Ferry, the same hills that Miles thought the Confederates would believe to be insurmountable. Skirmishes occurred over those days, but Miles believed he could hold out—that is until Jackson's guns began to bombard the town from the heights above, followed shortly after by an infantry attack by his most aggressive commander, fellow West Pointer A.P. Hill.

Though the fighting was heavy for a short time, Miles realized that the positioning of Jackson's guns and his advantage in numbers would eventually defeat the garrison. Still, critics say that Miles, aware that Lee was moving troops nearby, should have held out as long as possible in order to delay any possible rebel moves northward. As it was, McClellan, realizing that Harper's Ferry was likely to fall, had begun to move the bulk of his army in the direction of Harper's Ferry, either to relieve the town or to engage "Bobby" Lee (as McClellan called him) and defeat him once and for all. Should this happen, Lee was going to need Jackson's men, and Jackson was under orders to eliminate the threat of Harper's Ferry, leave a small garrison there, and then move with speed to rejoin the bulk of the Army of Northern Virginia.

Any extended period of time that Miles could hold out would have been useful, but after three days of Jackson maneuvering and placing his guns, the battle was essentially over in one day. Miles surrendered after his forces took minimal casualties; sadly, he was one of them, dying from complications from a terrible leg wound. The Confederate dead numbered less than 40, and the Union dead was just over that number, at 44. The Union losses altogether, though, were rather high, with 12,419 missing and/or taken prisoner.

While the Battle of Harper's Ferry was going on, McClellan was engaging the Confederates at South Mountain, which was to the northeast of Harper's Ferry by some twenty miles. In actuality, South Mountain was not really a peak; it was more of a heavily wooded ridge, which included three main "gaps" through which roads for local commerce passed.

On September 8th, 1862, Lee summoned his commanders and issued "Special Order 191." Lee emphasized security and warned his commanders against telling too many of their men about the plans contained in his order. His adjutant signed a number of copies in Lee's name for Jackson, Hill, and a handful of other commanders and had them distributed. One of Lee's officers—no one is completely sure who—wrapped them around three cigars to help keep them dry and at some point dropped them unknowingly.

The man who found them, Corporal Barton W. Mitchell of the 27th Indiana Volunteers, who would die after the war from the recurring infection from a wound sustained at Antietam, found the orders and relayed them to his chain of command, one of whom authenticated Lee's adjutant's signature, having known him well before the war. Lee's plans went all the way to the top, and when George McClellan received them, he exclaimed, "Now I know what to do! Here is a paper with which, if I cannot whip Bobby Lee, I will be willing to go home."

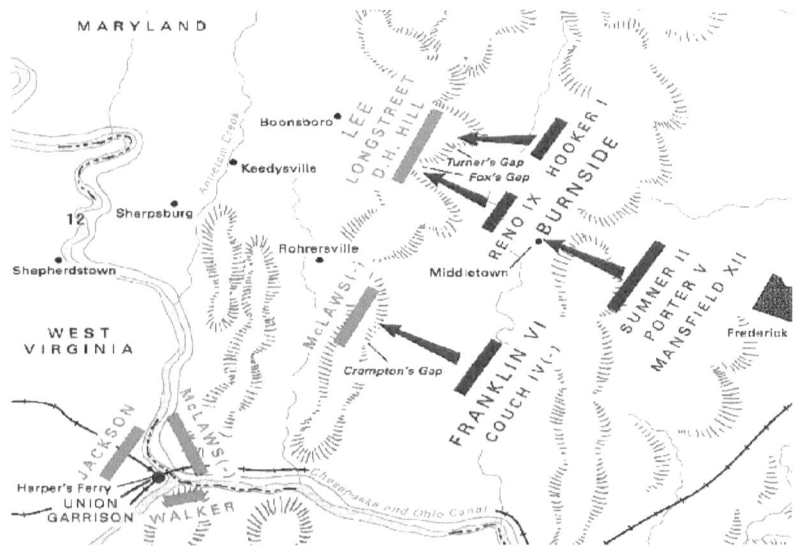

Illustration 8: Basic map of the Battles of South Mountain and Harper's Ferry. Note the location of Sharpsburg and Antietam Creek to the east.

Lee's forces at South Mountain were sparse, and the Confederate general's hope was for Jackson to defeat the garrison at Harper's Ferry and come to the aid of Lafayette McLaws and D.H. Hill, wherever they were engaged, when Jackson freed himself from his assault. In the days before, Lee had sent McLaws and Hill eastward to reconnoiter both a route north and to find and assess Federal forces in the area of Frederick, some ten miles east of South Mountain.

Another Confederate force, under General James Longstreet, had been sent north toward Pennsylvania with the aim of reaching Hagerstown, Maryland, just a few miles south of the Pennsylvania border. Longstreet was one of Lee's most trusted generals, and he had a reputation for his skill with artillery. Even more so than other famous Southern generals, Longstreet had good friends that ended up in the Union Army. His West Point roommate, William Rosecrans, became a prominent Union general, as did John Pope and George Henry Thomas (one of the best Union generals and who became known as the "Rock of Chickamauga" for his unyielding stance there). Longstreet was a party-goer at West Point, resulting in many demerits and graduation near the bottom of his class. Football, slovenliness, tardiness, and drinking seemed to have a priority, which may be one reason Longstreet was good friends with Ulysses S. Grant, whose wedding he attended in 1848. He practically had to because Grant's wife, Julia Dent, was Longstreet's cousin. Longstreet was also good friends with future Confederate commanders Lafayette McLaws, George Pickett, and D.H. Hill.

Though he graduated near the bottom of his West Point class in 1842, Longstreet was an able commander. Like the other generals mentioned in this book, he took part in the Mexican-American War, serving on the staff of future president Zachary Taylor. He took part in many actions but was most notable for rescuing a group of outnumbered Americans from a charge by two hundred Mexican lancers, cavalrymen who fought with lances. In the fight to take Mexico City, Longstreet was involved in desperate hand-to-hand combat. He ended the war with a brevet (temporary battlefield) promotion after he had led a charge at Chapultepec, in which he was wounded while carrying the colors. The man he handed the colors to was George Pickett.

Longstreet's Civil War record was distinguished both before and after the Battle of Antietam, and though he was defeated more than once, he took part in some of the great Confederate victories of the early war and helped Lee in his brilliant defense of Richmond in the war's later stages. At Gettysburg, he played a controversial role that is still debated by historians today, as he begged Lee to give up the battlefield and redeploy his men before the disastrous Pickett's Charge ended the Gettysburg Campaign.

Illustration 9: Longstreet during the war

As the Confederate men took their defensive positions in the gaps at South Mountain, Lee sent word for Longstreet to return to the area to reinforce them, as the rebel troops in the gaps were vastly outnumbered. When Longstreet's troops did arrive at 3:30 p.m. on September 12th, after having marched over rough terrain for nineteen hours to get there, they came just in time to allow the Southerners to begin a strongly fought tactical retreat to better ground.

The fighting at South Mountain, as you can see from the map above, took place at three gaps. North to south, they are Turner's Gap, Fox's Gap, and Crampton's Gap.

McClellan, who had pursued Lee rather slowly at this point, changed his pace when he received the lost Special Order 191. Having previously believed, as he was wont to do, that the majority of Confederate troops faced him directly, he now knew that Lee had divided his troops into three branches, and McClellan meant to take advantage of it.

On the morning of September 14th, Union division commander General Jacob D. Cox launched an attack on the right flank of the Southern troops at Fox's Gap. There, his Ohio division overran the North Carolinian troops of General Samuel Garland Jr., who was killed in action. After this, though, Cox stopped, waiting for further orders and allowing the Confederates to fortify their positions on the north flank of Fox's Gap.

To the north, General Ambrose Burnside, who openly admitted his lack of skill for greater command and who had turned down Lincoln's request to take command of the Army of the Potomac twice because of it, moved slowly and waited for orders from McClellan, who was slowly riding up the National Road (which led east-west from the coast through Virginia and Maryland) at the head of a large column of troops who cheered him on. Hearing that the battle was going on just a mile or two down the road, McClellan stopped his horse by the side of the road, tucked one hand in his jacket, and pointed toward the battle with the other hand. He remained that way for some time. It would have made a great statue, but many generals, including most Southern generals, would have been galloping toward the fighting and forcing their men into a trot. McClellan did neither of these things; instead, he gave general orders and presumed his subordinates would carry them out.

Burnside waited for one of his corps commanders, Joseph "Fightin' Joe" Hooker (who would replace Burnside as commander in chief when he accepted Lincoln's offer after Antietam), and at Fox's Gap, a usually aggressive Union general Jesse L. Reno moved slowly to reinforce the Union troops there.

At Crampton's Gap on the southern part of the mountain, 1,000 men of the CSA under General Howell Cobb faced 12,000 Union soldiers led by William B. Franklin, who, like his commander McClellan, believed he was facing more men than he actually was. Skirmishes took place most of the day until around 4 p.m. when Franklin's subordinate, Henry Slocum, got tired of waiting for his commander to give the order to advance with his whole force. Slocum led 12,000 Maine, New Jersey, Pennsylvania, and New York men right into the Southern position. At about that time, two regiments of Georgia troops showed up to reinforce Cobb, but it did no good.

Wave after wave of Union troops came at them relentlessly, and by nightfall, the position was taken. One rebel soldier, George Neese, a gunner in the horse artillery, said, "the Federals were so numerous that it looked as if they were creeping up out of the ground."

At the gaps to the north, the battle had been going on with some severity all day. At about the same time that Slocum led his men at Crampton's Gap, Longstreet's troops arrived in position. At the base of the mountain, they had met Robert E. Lee, who received their cheers and urged them on. The Texas Brigade, which had been led by the aggressive General John Bell Hood (a Kentuckian who joined the South when his state remained in the Union) until he had been arrested, demanded Lee reinstate Hood to command. "Give us Hood!" they shouted. Hood had been arrested and removed from command after the Second Battle of Bull Run in August over a conflict with another Confederate general over some captured wagons, and he was with Lee's entourage when the men confronted Lee about it. Lee replied, "You shall have him!" and called Hood forward. Lee asked Hood to express "regret" over the wagon incident, but Hood refused. Lee, being in a no-win situation, then replied, "Well, I will suspend your arrest until the impending battle is decided."

Toward dark, the Union generals had begun to pressure the Confederates at Fox's and Turner's Gaps after hard fighting among rocks, trees, and underbrush. Although the Southerners held their positions when the fighting ceased at full dark, Lee, Longstreet, and D.H. Hill met to discuss their options and decided that it was only a matter of time before their positions were overrun. Rather than risk complete defeat and possibly a panic-fueled rout, Lee elected to orderly retreat back toward Sharpsburg, between the Potomac River to the west and Antietam Creek. During the fighting at South Mountain, Lee had received word from Jackson about the fall of the Union garrison at Harper's Ferry. That evening, Lee sent word to Jackson to head toward Sharpsburg.

On the other side, George McClellan sent word back to his wife, saying he had won a "glorious victory." A similar message went to Washington, DC. Lincoln responded, "God bless you and all with you. Destroy the rebel army if possible."

Chapter 5 – Antietam

Illustration 10: Disposition of troops morning 9/15/1862

Despite the setback at South Mountain, Lee was still determined to fight on Northern ground. He knew McClellan was cautious, but Lee also knew that he wasn't stupid and that if the Southern generals weren't careful, "Little Mac" might be able to wrangle the decisive victory he had been looking for.

Even with that knowledge, Lee decided to take up a dangerous position near Sharpsburg, a small town whose population today is only about 800. It was roughly the same in 1862. Behind Sharpsburg is the Potomac River, one of the widest on the North American continent. The river near Sharpsburg is not nearly as wide as it is near Washington, DC, but it is wide enough that Lee, if he and his forces were bottled up in the area, would probably only have one bridge with which to remove his army. If that were the case, and the Federal forces were on his heels, the Army of Northern Virginia would be shot to pieces.

But one thing that even the laziest of history students know is that Robert E. Lee was a gambler. Aside from that, the area did afford some defensive advantages. Sharpsburg itself was essentially in the middle of Lee's lines. The Potomac protected Lee's rear if McClellan attempted a wide flanking move; however, Lee and the entire country knew McClellan would not attempt such a move.

Antietam Creek ran from north to south in Lee's front. Many would actually call the creek a small river, and though there were places that were shallow enough for a man to cross in waist-deep water, three main bridges spanned the waterway.

A mile and a half or so above Sharpsburg was a series of woods, punctuated by farm fields on rolling hills. These were thick woods, which blocked one's vision and sound to some degree. As you can see from the map, they were named for where they lay—north, east, and west. The rebels positioned themselves around the West Woods, using the Dunker Church as a base of operations and an anchor point for their defense. The church was so named for a pacifist sect that baptized their congregants by "dunking" them, rather than using the more common method of pouring water on the head.

From north to south ran the Hagerstown Pike, the main roadway north that linked the larger town of Hagerstown to Sharpsburg, which was thirteen miles away. To the south of the woods and the Dunker Church, just to the east of the Hagerstown Pike, was the "Sunken Road," so-called because the wear and tear on the dirt surface had caused it to sink below the level of the ground around it. The Sunken Road was bordered on both sides in spots by a split-rail fence. After the battle, and to this day, the Sunken Road has been referred to as "Bloody Lane."

Illustration 11: "Bloody Lane" immediately after the battle

In the south, just outside Sharpsburg and near to Antietam Creek, was another Southern force, with Lafayette McLaws and R.H Anderson in reserve. Later in the day, the action in this area would be remembered for the slaughter that took place on the southernmost bridge over Antietam Creek. Then known as Rohrbach's Bridge, today it's known as Burnside's Bridge, for the Union general whose troops forced their way across it, taking immense casualties.

The battlefield of Antietam has been preserved and today resembles in many ways the field as it looked on that September day in 1862—rolling hills, cornfields, orchards, and fences, some of which gave cover and some which didn't

Illustration 12: Dunker Church now and then

Chapter 6 – Dunker Church

One of the contributing factors in the large casualty count at Antietam was the confusion and lack of communication that took place, mostly on the Union side. There were also some unfortunate/fortunate (depending on whose side you were on) accidents, which made things even more confusing and bloody. To describe each unit action and maneuver that took place throughout the battle would require much more space than we have here. What follows is a general overview of the battle in the north around the Dunker Church and what had become known as simply the "Cornfield."

At 5:30 a.m., in the far north of the battlefield, Union General Joseph Hooker ordered three divisions to move out. General Abner Doubleday (the supposed inventor of baseball, although that claim, which Doubleday never made himself, has been discredited by modern-day historians) was on the right, General George Meade (who would lead the Union to victory the next summer at Gettysburg) was in the center, and on the left was General James Ricketts, another West Pointer and native New Yorker. The first two columns moved through the North Woods, and the last made their way to the East Woods.

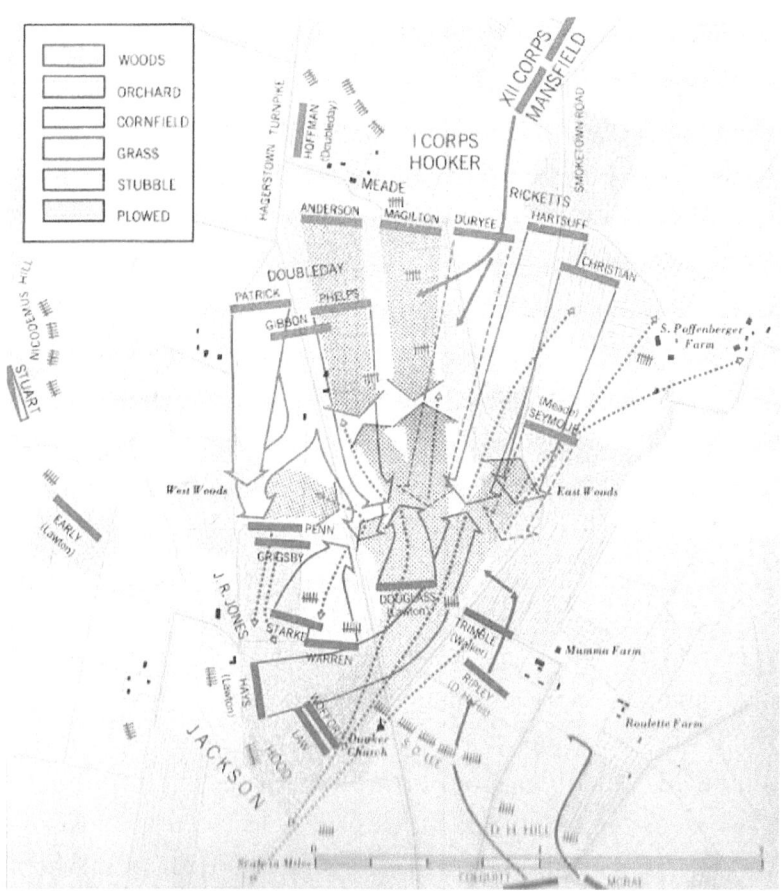

Illustration 13: The battle in the north near the Dunker Church and the Cornfield

As soon as Doubleday's men emerged from the North Woods, Confederate guns opened fire. The rebels were so accurate that they didn't have to fire many shots to find the right range, as their second shell tore into the 6th Wisconsin Brigade, killing two men and wounding eleven. Within a few seconds, Federal guns to the rear and on the flanks opened up, and a raging artillery duel began. Not only did the guns near the Hagerstown Pike and the advanced rebel lines open fire, but so did the guns on the rise near the Dunker Church. These were eight cannons from Jeb Stuart's forces, a dozen from Jackson, and another sixteen from batteries across the road from the church. Generally speaking, Confederate batteries consisted of four guns, while Federal units consisted of six.

The Union guns then joined the fray. Two miles away, across Antietam Creek, 24 heavy Federal guns opened fire. A journalist nearby attempted to count the blasts of these guns, which amounted to about sixty rounds per minute.

This was when five Pennsylvania regiments marched to the south of the East Woods and into the right side of the rebel line in front of the church. The Southern unit in this area was commanded by Colonel James Walker—the same man who had challenged Stonewall Jackson to a duel some years before. Walker was wounded and had to be taken from the field, but his men put up such a fight that the "Bluecoats" retreated.

General Joseph Hooker moved with his men toward the Dunker Church and the cornfield north and east of it. In that cornfield, Hooker and his men saw glinting Confederate bayonets among the stalks. So, he called up more guns, and six batteries opened fire on the cornfield, which was from now on known to men on both sides and history as *the* Cornfield. In his battlefield report, Hooker wrote, "every stalk of corn in the northern and greater part of the field was cut as closely as could have been done with a knife, and the slain lay in rows precisely as they had stood in their ranks a few minutes before."

Hooker called for reinforcements to press on, and on the Union left, General Rickett's 1st Brigade filed out of the East Woods and into the eastern part of the Cornfield, where stalks of corn still partially hid their advance, as well as what was waiting for them on the other side. Because the maneuvers and communications of the time required officers to be able to see and identify units personally, most flew the national flag and the flag of their unit(s). This was what the Union men did, and the Georgia unit waiting for them saw their flags coming at them through the corn. At about two hundred yards, the Georgians opened fire, which was then returned by the men in blue.

Two of the Union men in the Cornfield were brothers, German immigrants named Gleasman. One went down after being shot by a rebel sharpshooter some distance away. This was seen by his brother, who pointed and said, "There is the man who killed my brother, and he is taking aim now against that tree." At just that moment, he, too, was felled by the same man, falling next to his brother on the field.

From about 6 to 6:45 a.m., both sides poured in reinforcements to the area. At 6:45, Walker's unit, who had lost 40 percent of its men, began to retreat. The Georgians next to them remained, but they had taken even more punishment—a 50 percent casualty rate, and their commander had been killed, as had five Confederate unit commanders in the area.

As the gray line of Confederates was about to give, another rebel unit rushed into the fight, the Louisiana Brigade, which consisted of men mainly from New Orleans who were known as the "Tigers" (yes, the Louisiana Tigers—history is everywhere, LSU fans). These men charged into the Federal lines and drove them back toward the East Woods. One Union officer writing after the war called it, "the most deadly fire of the war...the dead and wounded go down in scores." To break up the Tigers' assault, Federal cannons were quickly brought to bear on the advancing Louisiana men, blowing the Tigers to pieces at point-blank range. Those who survived were then attacked by General Rickett's last reserve brigade. The fighting then shifted to hand-to-hand combat, at one point fighting over fallen Union colors. In trying to retrieve them, seven of ten men from the 90th Pennsylvania died. Private William Paul grabbed the colors and made it safely back to Union lines, and he won the newly established Medal of Honor for his actions. In the conflict near the East Woods, the units had lost nearly 50 percent of their strength.

At the same time as this was happening near the East Woods, the Union forces were pushing into the West Woods on the rebels' left. As they were coming down the western side of the Hagerstown Pike, they came under fire from still more men in the Cornfield. The

Federal soldiers brought up cannons to deal with this, but as the guns were setting up, rebel sharpshooters began to pick their crews off. Within five minutes, more than half of the Union crews were dead or wounded.

Throughout the morning, in many different parts of the Cornfield on both sides of the Hagerstown Pike, unit after unit was thrown into the fighting. Wisconsin units and men were mixed in with New York units and men, and by about 6:45 a.m., they were about halfway to the Dunker Church.

As this happened, another Confederate counterattack occurred out of the West Woods. There, Brigadier General William Starke had the men from his two brigades line up along a wooden rail fence just thirty yards away from the Federal flank. In turn, some of the men from Wisconsin and New York wheeled right (think of a swinging door), and an artillery unit to the north opened up on the rebels. Within fifteen minutes, the rebels were reeling, and their commander was struck by three Minié balls and soon died. All along that fence line and into the Union position were dead and dying men, but the fighting raged on.

In the small "no man's land" between the two enemies, Confederate Captain R.P. Jennings lay wounded with another man. The two men argued about what the safest course would be—to try to run or remain where they were, as bullets were landing all around them. "I may as well be killed running as lying still," Jennings said, and he got up and amazingly made it back to the rebel lines.

All along the Pike, the men in gray were falling back toward the Dunker Church. These were Jackson's men, and many of the units had taken 50 percent casualties or more. Just when it looked like the Confederate left might break, 2,300 men in gray came tearing through a hole in the churchyard fence and toward the fighting, screaming their rebel yell, that unique battle cry of the South, which is explained generally by historian Shelby Foote in Ken Burns' miniseries *The Civil War* as a howl and a series of yips. These were the men of John

Bell Hood's division, the Texas Brigade, and they were angry. The night before, Stonewall Jackson had promised them that they would be held in reserve and given time to eat a real meal, which they had not done in days. That morning, as they set up their fires and pots and got ready to sit down to eat, the call came for them to join the fighting.

No man likes having his breakfast interrupted, least of all when he hasn't really eaten in days and especially when he is being called on to perhaps go and die. So, they gathered their arms and ran into battle, surging through the churchyard and into the Cornfield, across the Pike and toward the East Woods. Hood himself followed, trying to maneuver his horse so that he didn't tread on some wounded man, for the field was almost invisible under the bodies.

The Texans pushed every Federal soldier in their path out of the way, sending them into a panic–at least those they didn't shoot down. Hood's Texans were soon joined by D.H. Hill's division, but the Texans took the brunt of the fighting in the Cornfield on the eastern side of the Hagerstown Pike. Barreling out of the field, Union men who had fought well all morning gave way to Hood. A Union private, no more than sixteen, stood on a knoll and tried to rally his comrades, yelling, "Rally, boys, rally! Die like men, don't run like dogs!"

Jackson sent a messenger to Hood, who replied back to Stonewall, saying that he would soon be pressed back unless he received reinforcements but that he would keep pressing until he no longer could. When the fighting did end, the 1st Texas Brigade was found to have sustained 186 men dead out of 226, an 82.3 percent casualty rate, the highest for any regiment throughout the costly war.

Back along the Pike to the west, the Federal units left in the area banded together and began to fire on the surging rebels on the other side of the road. Farther to the west, Confederate General Jubal Early's men were marching toward the Pike. Some Union guns fired westward, while others fired east. Forty out of one hundred of the battery's men were wounded or killed that morning. Other men jumped in to keep the guns firing, including General John Gibbon, the commander of the Federal center unit. One gun was positioned right in the middle of the road, and Gibbon noticed it was firing too high. He jumped down from his horse, lowered the elevation of the gun himself, and gave the order to fire through the wooden rails of the fence and into the rebels who were on the other side. At least a dozen enemy soldiers were blown to pieces by the canister shot. After the battle, a Union officer said he saw an arm fly thirty feet through the air.

The men in Gibbon's battery increased their firepower to double canister. Think of a shotgun switching from .20 gauge to .12 gauge or even .10 gauge. Three Confederate charges attempted to overtake the guns, and all three times they were beaten back. This took place between fifteen and twenty minutes. The Union men were soon going to be out of ammunition, and so, Gibbon called for a retreat. A total of 26 dead and mangled horses lay around the cannon, but the remaining Union men in blue found enough animals to limber (mount for traveling) their guns, and they made their way off the field while being under fire the whole time. They retreated, along with much of Joe Hooker's division, about three-quarters of a mile back toward Poffenberger's Farm, as you can see on the map above. Hood's men retreated themselves back to the West Woods. Seeing so few men with their general, a Southern officer asked Hood, "Where is your division?" Foreshadowing the comments made after Pickett's Charge at Gettysburg, which would happen around a year later, Hood replied, "Dead on the field." Hood, a man noted for his aggression and who would become even more famous for it later in the war, said that Antietam was the fiercest fighting he had ever seen.

But it was only 7:30 in the morning, and the battle had been raging for about an hour. Hundreds were already dead and wounded, but only a small segment of both forces had been in action. There were still units to the south that had not been engaged at all.

After all of this fighting, the Union side still had reserves to throw into the battle, the troops led by General Joseph Mansfield. At 58, he was old for the time, and he had never led large groups of men in battle. Although he was a West Pointer and a veteran of the Mexican-American War, most of his career had been spent behind a desk or performing engineering duties. Worse still, his XII Corps was made up of many soldiers who had never seen battle and had little training. To try to keep some control of his rookie troops and to increase the force with which he hit the rebels, Mansfield ordered his men into very tightly bunched formations as they marched to battle at the center of the Union line. Other officers tried to dissuade him, arguing that this would increase casualties from Confederate artillery, but Mansfield would hear none of it.

As his men approached the East Woods, they came under fire. Mansfield then tried to maneuver his men into a firing formation. This took time, which made the situation even worse. At one point, Mansfield told one unit, the 10th Maine, to stop firing, as he believed their targets to be Union men. As his men protested, Mansfield took a fatal shot in the chest. His executive officer took command and finally got the men moving. And down toward the Cornfield they went.

That cornfield was only about 250 yards deep and about 400 yards wide, but in it were hundreds of bodies, both dead and wounded. That day, the Cornfield changed hands *fifteen times*. In an attempt to take over the Cornfield, the brigades of the XII Corps engaged with men of D.H. Hill's unit, men who had loaded their guns with "buck and ball" cartridges, which is a ball surround by pieces of buckshot. Most men that were hit by these shots did not die, but the wounded covered the battlefield.

Finally, at about 8:30 a.m., another Union force, led by General George Greene (a grandson of Revolutionary War hero Nathanael Greene), came marching from the northeast to flank the rebel position. Seeing a huge force of Federals marching their way, the battle-weary rebels in the Cornfield began to break. Another of Greene's brigades moved even farther south to attempt to turn the Confederate right flank. Soon, they were within sight of the Dunker

Church, which had been the Union goal all morning. Greene's men were advancing toward the church so quickly, though, that he had to call a halt to their advance. His artillery was lagging behind, and unless they caught up, the advance would be pushed back. Greene called his men to a halt by calling out, "Halt, 102nd! You are bully boys but don't go any farther!"

As his artillery caught up, Greene ordered a charge and drove the last Confederate battery off of the plateau near where the Dunker Church stood. Some Union men cautiously peeked into the windows of the church, but they saw nothing but wounded rebels lying on the pews.

By this point, the Union held most of the area east of the Hagerstown Pike and had some troops in the West Woods, but there still were rebels in the woods as well. The lines in the north ended about two hundred yards east of the Dunker Church, and at about 9 a.m., the fighting on the northern part of the battlefield ended. It had been a slaughterhouse, but the day was still young.

Chapter 7: "Bloody Lane"

Antietam was chaotic. A thousand movements of units large and small were fighting over the same ground, as they had in the Cornfield. However, if one was to see the battle unfold from above, one would see that the struggle unfolded rather neatly, if that can be said about a battle in which thousands died. The fighting began in the north, near the Dunker Church and the Cornfield, then it flared up in the center, and the fighting ended in the southern end of the battlefield.

The next phase of the battle was no less bloody. In fact, as you can see from the title, this aspect of the battle was dominated by the struggle along what has become known to history as simply the "Bloody Lane."

The fighting in the center began almost by accident. A Union brigade under General William French had become separated from its division that was headed south, away from the fighting in the Cornfield area. The commanding general of the II Corps sent his son as a runner to find them, and when he did, he relayed his father's order that rather than moving back north to rejoin the rest of the corps, they should attack the Confederate center lines near a side road that headed straight east from the Hagerstown Pike.

French confronted men from D.H. Hill's division, which was a part of General James Longstreet's corps and who had seen three of five brigades torn to pieces in the fighting alongside the Pike. Now the rest of Hill's division would be involved in another bloody engagement of the Civil War.

Though Hill's 2,500 men were outnumbered by French's division, they possessed what in 19th-century parlance was "good ground." They sat atop a small gradual ridge in the road mentioned earlier—which had been sunken from years of traffic—with rail fences lining most of both sides of the road. For the rebels, this was a gift, as it was a trench they didn't have to dig, and the men from French's division were coming right at them. At this point in the battle, the men faced each other rifle to rifle, bayonet to bayonet, but no cannons were brought up until the fighting began to rage.

At 9:30 a.m., French attacked the Sunken Road, and men began to be cut down in rows, falling like cornstalks under the scythe. Most of the men in this attack were recruits that had never seen action. The second Union attack, just minutes later, was also made up of recruits, but they managed to beat back a counterattack by a brigade of Alabamians, who really should not have left the protection of the Sunken Road. Yet another attack, this time by three veteran divisions, was also stopped, the men mown down in action. Within about fifty minutes, French's division had suffered 30 percent losses.

Leaders on both sides soon realized that the battle had shifted south, and so, they sent more and more units to the area around the Sunken Road. Robert E. Lee sent over 3,000 men under Major General Richard H. Anderson to aid Hill and move his line farther to the right (eastward) in the hopes that they could envelop French's attacking division. Simultaneously, another 4,000 Union men moved in under Major General Israel B. Richardson to prevent French's division from being surrounded.

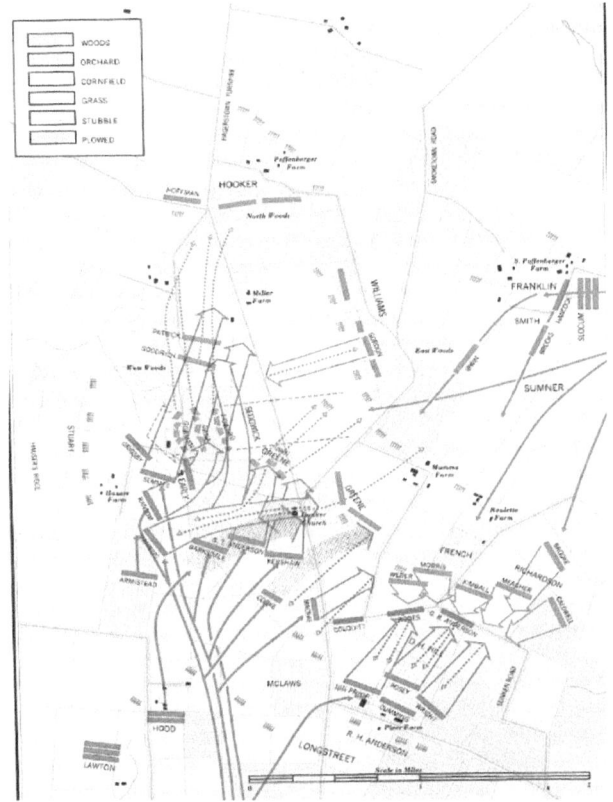

As soon as they arrived, the Union men launched their attack, the fourth on the Confederate position in an hour. In the vanguard was a brigade of Irish immigrants led by Thomas Meagher. Facing them on the other side were Irish immigrants in Hill's division. The Union Irish would suffer about 50 percent casualties before falling back.

At noon, the fifth Union attack began to push the rebels back. A number of Confederate officers had been killed or wounded in the fighting, and with their loss, the integrity of the rebel units began to break down. Finally, a unit of New Yorkers managed to flank the far right of the Southern line and fire down at them from a small knoll. Between the firing from their front and now from their left, the Southerners at the easternmost part of the road were slaughtered. As the rebels began to flee, artillery, personally led by General Longstreet, began to open fire on the pursuing Union men, breaking up their attack. A counterattack by the remnants of D.H. Hill's division almost succeeded in outflanking the Union left around the knoll, but the damage was done. Both sides were exhausted. In the fighting that took place there from about 9:30 a.m. to 1 p.m., a total of 5,600 casualties were sustained by both sides, with the Union suffering a bit more.

As the Confederates were moving away from the Sunken Road (already known as the "Bloody Lane" by this point), some of McClellan's officers urged him to throw in some men from his reserves, which numbered over twenty thousand infantry and cavalry. McClellan took the advice of Commander Edwin Sumner of the II Corps and remained in place. The advice of this corps commander likely reinforced McClellan's already cautious nature.

Still, the day was not over. Another part of the battlefield was about to erupt in the south, and it would be no less a slaughter than what had already occurred.

Illustration 14: Attack of the Irish at Bloody Lane from a painting by Jeremy Scott

Chapter 8: Burnside's Bridge

When General Ambrose Burnside is remembered today, it is sadly during trivia contests about where the word "sideburns" comes from. However, Burnside and the men under his command should be remembered for the effort they gave in the Civil War, for it was a matter of life, death, and freedom.

As we have mentioned, General Burnside was a mediocre general, and he knew it. Burnside was better fitted for a lesser command than corps commander or commander of the army. That doesn't mean he did not give his all in the struggle because he did. It's just that, unfortunately, his all wasn't all that good.

Burnside's career was really a tragedy in many ways. He was a major player in the First Battle of Bull Run and took part in the ignominious retreat from that battlefield. He also played a major role at Antietam, which we will tell you about momentarily. After Antietam, Burnside was given command of the Army of the Potomac when Lincoln fired McClellan, and his first major battle with the Army of the Potomac was the Union slaughter at Fredericksburg in December 1862. After that, he, too, was fired and sent to the West, first to Kentucky, which was a quiet area, and then he took part (with some success) in the campaigns in Tennessee. This brought Burnside back to Virginia, where, again, he did not distinguish himself and was partially responsible for the disaster of the Battle of the Crater during the greater Siege of Petersburg in 1864. After the war, Burnside became a US senator, successful industrialist, and the first president of the National Rifle Association. But this was all in the future of the man who was supposed to take over a key bridge crossing Antietam Creek.

George McClellan's original plan was for the southern part of his armies to move against the men in gray in a diversionary attack to support the Union effort in the northern part of the battlefield, but a number of factors changed this plan.

Firstly, the orders for Burnside to launch his attack did not reach the bearded general until 10 a.m., by which time the battle in the north had been going on for some four bloody hours.

Second, the relationship between Burnside and McClellan had been strained for the past few days. They had been great friends since West Point when they were teenagers. McClellan had even helped Burnside out financially when they were in the private sector before the war. Now, McClellan had chastised his friend for moving too slowly, both in the lead-up to South Mountain and in the battle itself. A warning from McClellan that one was too cautious could be interpreted in a number of ways, but either way, a rebuke from the cautious "Little Mac" that one was being too careful was not a good sign.

Burnside also resented the changes in command structure that McClellan had recently instituted, which were in effect at Antietam. In essence, Burnside was formally acting as McClellan's second-in-command, in charge of both his own IX Corps and Joseph Hooker's I Corps. Before the battle, McClellan had changed this so that Burnside was only in command of his own corps, which, in truth, was an improvement and should have allowed his orders to be acted upon more swiftly. Whether this affected Burnside at Antietam or not, we cannot be sure, but the strain between the generals did affect those around Burnside, as they were not sure exactly what the chain of command was.

No matter what time Burnside's orders arrived or at what time he chose to move, one thing was clear: his task was not going to be easy. His front faced Antietam Creek, which in many places was too deep to ford. Three bridges crossed the creek in its run through the battlefield. Burnside's men were facing the southernmost bridge, known as Rohrbach's Bridge, which was named after a farmer in the area. However, there were fordable places in the area, and the plan was for the Union men to cross the bridge in a frontal assault on Confederate positions that could be easily seen, as well as across Snavely's Ford about a mile to the south. It was hoped that the ford would either have no defenders or would be lightly defended so that the Federal forces could swing around and trap the rebels in a pincer move. At least, that was the plan.

During the morning, while waiting for McClellan's orders to arrive, Burnside and his second-in-command, Brigadier General Jacob Cox, looked at the bridge and the land directly across from it. Neither man thought to check out the ground on either side of it or the depth of the water there. In places not so far away, the creek was waist-deep or a bit less. They knew it would not be easy to cross, but it would not be as difficult as marching directly across a bridge into the face of enemy cannons.

The bridge was an arched, stone structure (which has today been restored to its pre-war appearance) just wide enough for four men to cross in a line abreast. The sides of the bridge were about waist high. In other words, any man crossing that bridge was a sitting duck. If used in conjunction with one or two concurrent crossings of the shallow parts of the creek nearby, moving across the bridge might not go too horribly. However, that is not what happened that morning.

Illustration 15: Burnside's Bridge today

Burnside had 12,500 men and 50 cannons on his side of the bridge. Had he acted sooner in the morning, he might have won the day for the Union much earlier and saved countless lives. But he did not get his orders, was a cautious man by nature, and his reconnaissance was sorely lacking. If his scouts had been more on top of things, Burnside would have realized that Robert E. Lee had stripped the southern end of his front to reinforce the men fighting in the Cornfield and Bloody Lane.

Facing Burnside in the south were five weakened brigades, which consisted of about two to three thousand men in total, along with twelve cannons. Immediately in the area of the bridge were about four hundred men with six to eight guns. It is a military axiom that an attacker should have at least a two to one advantage. Burnside had a five or six to one advantage, but that was partially negated by the ground on the other side of the bridge. There was a high wooded bluff there that used to be the side of an old quarry, and therefore, in addition to the trees and large boulders, it provided excellent cover and vantage points.

The Southern general in command at the bridge was Brigadier General Robert Toombs of Georgia, a successful politician who was the first Confederate secretary of state. After Fort Sumter, he warned Jefferson Davis, the president of the Confederacy, that war should be averted, accurately perceiving the Union's reaction to conflict. "Mr. President, at this time it is suicide, murder, and will lose us every friend at the North. You will wantonly strike a hornet's nest which extends from mountain to ocean, and legions now quiet will swarm out and sting us to death. It is unnecessary; it puts us in the wrong; it is fatal."

Toombs had become disenchanted with some of his superiors, many of whom were West Point men, and he made no secret about it. Toombs felt them to be overly cautious. By the time of the Battle of Antietam, Toombs had determined that his military career would end once he distinguished himself in a great battle. In a letter to his wife, he said, "The day after such an event, I will retire if I live through it."

So, Toombs awaited what he could see was going to be an overwhelming number of Union troops. Leading south away from the bridge and toward Snavely's Ford was a dirt road, which was also in relatively plain view of the rebels on the western side of the river. If and when the Union men decided to flank the bridge, Southern sharpshooters would be able to line them up perfectly.

Behind the bridge and toward Sharpsburg, there were another twelve rebel cannons, and just east of the town were another small number of guns. The plateau where the guns were positioned would soon be called "Cemetery Hill." These guns were firing at other locations on the battlefield just a little before 10 a.m. when an aide from McClellan galloped up to Burnside with orders to advance. The orders had been written at 9:10 a.m.–fifty minutes before. This was at the time of the rebel repulse of Hooker's troops in the north and while Federal troops were getting beaten back in the West Woods. McClellan had waited until he received word from his reserve VI Corps that they were marching up to the southern end of the battlefield to provide the added punch to break through the rebel lines once Burnside's men had crossed the bridge.

The honor (and it was an honor, at least to the officers in charge) of leading the first assault across the bridge was given to the Kanawha Division, which was made up of mostly Ohio men who had distinguished themselves at the Battle of South Mountain.

But before the Ohioans could try to storm across the bridge, the 11th Connecticut Regiment was going to try to take control of the bridge by moving out onto the span and laying down enough fire on the rebels for the Ohioans to advance. Having received their orders from behind the crest of a hill, the Ohioans began to climb. As soon as the 11th crested the hill, the Confederates opened fire.

Two companies moved to the right and two to the left. The men on the right were pinned down right away, but the men on the left, who were also under heavy fire, reached the road that ran parallel to the creek. Part of the regiment went down to the creek to see if they could cross on foot, but the water was four feet deep, and the current was strong and clearly in the view of the rebel riflemen, who opened fire on the men in the water. The 11th sustained 30 percent casualties in fifteen minutes.

The 11th's commander, Colonel Henry Kingsbury, attempted to lead his men on a charge across the bridge, but the Union men could not make any headway, and their highly regarded colonel was killed. Things only got worse from there.

The commander of the Kanawha Division, who was leading his men to the bridge, somehow got lost. Later it was discovered that neither he nor any of his officers had examined the ground they were supposed to take to the bridge, and so, instead of simply cresting the bridge as the 11th had done, they veered to the north for a quarter of a mile, under fire almost the whole time.

All this time, the men in the division commanded by Brigadier General Isaac Rodman were finding the going tough in their journey to reach Snavely's Ford to the south. Once again, the officers in charge had listened to their scouts but had not examined the ground, as the route to the ford was overgrown with brambles, rocks, and trees.

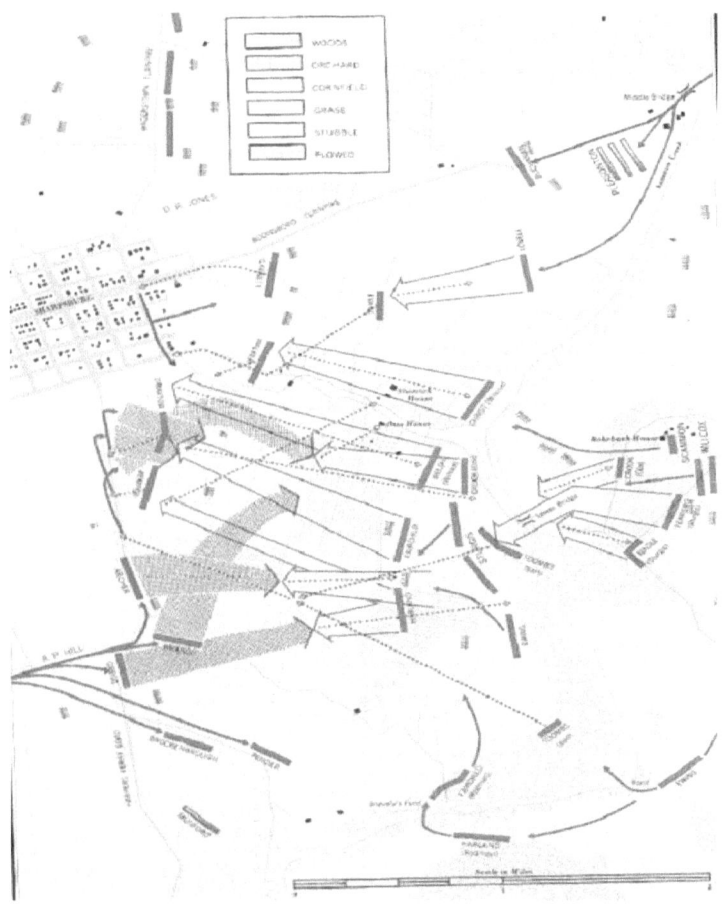

Illustration 16: Movements after the Union crossing of Burnside's Bridge

Next up at the bridge were two regiments, the 2nd Maryland and 6th New Hampshire. They, too, were stopped in their tracks with heavy casualties. All the while, McClellan, whose headquarters was some distance away, sent more orders to Burnside after already having sent several messages urging him to cross the bridge. The fourth said, "Tell him if it costs 10,000 men he must go now." When the fourth aide arrived, Burnside exploded on him, saying, "McClellan appears to think I am not trying my best to carry this bridge; you are the third or fourth one who has been to me this morning with similar orders."

Attempt number three began at 12:30 p.m. The brigade commander, Colonel Edward Ferrero, had been an etiquette and dance instructor at West Point and was a corrupt Tammany Hall politician from New York City before the war. He wasn't a soldier, but two of his regiments, the 51st New York and the 51st Pennsylvania, were good—as were their unit commanders. With his men assembled around him, Ferrero received a runner from Burnside, who told him, "It is General Burnside's special request that the two 51st's take that bridge. Will you do it?" Ferrero's men were upset—they did not want to follow their commander across. Aside from being a bad soldier, Ferrero had recently suspended their whiskey ration. One of the soldiers yelled, "Will you give us our whiskey, Colonel, if we take it?" He answered, "Yes, by God, as much as you want!" That did the trick.

However, promise of whiskey or not, the 51sts had a hard time taking the bridge. They hunkered down behind sections of stone wall near the bridge and tore apart sections of rail fence, piling them up for cover, all while under heavy fire. After half an hour of intense fire, the men of the 51sts noticed the shots were slowing down. The weight of Union numbers, as well as their own casualties and slowly disappearing ammunition, forced the Confederates to begin an orderly withdrawal. A Union captain, who was joined by two color-bearers and their guard, moved onto the bridge. As they were halfway across, the Union men saw the last remaining Confederates running to the rear.

The Union had the bridge, but it came at a high cost. They suffered 500 casualties to the Georgians' 150. Additionally, three hours had gone by, which Robert E. Lee used to summon reinforcements from other sections of the battlefield. And General A.P. Hill's division had just arrived after a seventeen-mile march from Harper's Ferry.

Making matters worse, after the bridge was taken and a foothold had been secured on the other side, Burnside's officers made another blunder. They hadn't brought ammunition across the bridge with them, at least not enough to sustain an assault on the rebel positions just outside Sharpsburg. Over the next two hours, a traffic jam ensued. Wagons, cannons, horses, and men were all moving this way and that on the narrow bridge. All the while, Robert E. Lee was preparing another welcome for the Union men.

At 2:30, A.P. Hill's 3,000 men arrived on the field. Lee positioned them on his right flank, which extended northeastward to the Boonsboro Pike. On the Pike itself, Union troops under General Robert C. Buchanan held a position to block any rebel movement in the center but didn't dare advance close to Sharpsburg, as the area around the road was open to fire from both sides. Worse still for the Federals, the ground moving toward the town and away from the creek was sloped, and the rebels had the high ground.

At 3 p.m., Burnside gave the order. For the next two and a half hours, the Union assaulted the rebel positions. Fighting was particularly intense (not that it was not intense all along the line) in the area near the Otto House and the Sherrick House, along a small creek that ran to the Antietam Creek.

By 5:30, the rebels had had enough. In the time since the end of the war, much has been said about the bravery and passion of the Southern troops, and they surely had it. However, it should be remembered that the men in blue had it as well, as they walked essentially into the mouth of Hell, directly into the rebel guns, and despite taking thirty, forty, and fifty percent casualties, they continued to attack until the battle was theirs.

Unfortunately, at the time, the Union armies were led by men who were not ready for the decisive action that was needed to claim total victory. In Sharpsburg that evening, civilians hunkered down in basements or fled the town in panic. Many rebel soldiers expected the Federals to arrive at any minute. Once the sun went down, however,

Lee and the other rebel commanders were relatively sure that no more Union attacks would take place, though they made themselves ready in case it happened.

McClellan had over 12,000 men yet to see battle. He could have moved them past his exhausted soldiers and likely taken the town. McClellan might have ended the war by trapping Lee and his army on the eastern side of the Potomac. But he was convinced, once again, that Lee had more men than he really did and that the "wily silver fox" (as many referred to Lee) was planning a counterattack at any moment.

Lee had no such attack planned. The next day, there was a short truce arranged to remove the injured men from the field and exchange the wounded that had been taken as prisoner. That evening, Lee began his withdrawal back into Virginia, and the war would go on for two and a half more years.

Conclusion

The Battle of Antietam remains the bloodiest single-day battle in American military history. Lincoln, his Cabinet, and virtually everyone in the Union were sickened at the cost. Though he and his men spun the battle as a Union victory, which it technically was, everyone knew that a huge opportunity had been lost and that likely thousands of men had died for nothing.

That was all except for George McClellan, who was sure he had won a great victory and prevented Lee from launching another assault into the North. Once again, he was wrong. Lincoln waited until the midterm elections to fire McClellan, as the general had powerful allies and was well-liked by his troops. Besides that, the president could use McClellan's recognized organizational powers to help the army recover after the battle. But in November, McClellan was done, never to return.

The casualties in the battle were as follows: 12,410 Union, including 2,108 dead, with the Confederate casualties at 10,316 with 1,546 dead. People were still finding bleached bones of unburied bodies years later.

There was one positive that came out of the Battle of Antietam. On New Year's Day 1863, Lincoln issued the Emancipation Proclamation.

> That on the first day of January, in the year of our Lord one thousand eight hundred and sixty-three, all persons held as slaves within any State or designated part of a State, the

people whereof shall then be in rebellion against the United States, shall be then, thenceforward, and forever free.

However, historians will tell you that, in effect, the Emancipation Proclamation really did not do anything at all. The slaves mentioned were not in the Union's border states (slave states that had declared their support for the Union), and nothing Lincoln could say would free the states "then in rebellion." Still, the Civil War was about freedom, and the Emancipation Proclamation let the South know that the war would continue until they were defeated. The Emancipation Proclamation was a necessary step in the eventual passing of the Thirteenth Amendment to the Constitution, which was passed shortly before Lincoln's assassination and abolished the practice of slavery.

Here's another book by Captivating History that you might be interested in

Free Bonus from Captivating History (Available for a Limited time)

Hi History Lovers!

Now you have a chance to join our exclusive history list so you can get your first history ebook for free as well as discounts and a potential to get more history books for free! Simply visit the link below to join.

Captivatinghistory.com/ebook

Also, make sure to follow us on Facebook, Twitter and Youtube by searching for Captivating History.

References

Bailey, Ronald H. THE BLOODIEST DAY: THE BATTLE OF ANTIETAM. Time Life Education, 1984.

Foote, Shelby. THE CIVIL WAR: A NARRATIVE: VOLUME 2: FREDERICKSBURG TO MERIDIAN. New York: Vintage, 2011.

McPherson, James M. BATTLE CRY OF FREEDOM: THE CIVIL WAR ERA. New York: Oxford University Press, 2003.

www.ingramcontent.com/pod-product-compliance
Lightning Source LLC
LaVergne TN
LVHW041650060526
838200LV00040B/1785